D1756791

The Last Mountain
The Life of Robert Wood
by
Violet Sigoloff Flume

Published By
Branden Press Inc.
Box 843 • 21 Station St.
Brookline Village, MA 02147

ISBN 0-8283-1829-8 (cloth)
ISBN 0-8283-1878-6 (paper)

Library of Congress Cataloging in Publication Data

Flume, Violet Sigoloff.
  The last mountain.

  1. Wood, Robert W. (Robert William), 1889-1979.
2. Painters – United States – Biography. I. Wood,
Robert W. (Robert William), 1889-1979. II. Title
ND237.W797F58   1983   759.13 [B]   82-22632
ISBN 0-8283-1829-8

Dedication

To Florence Wood Brumaghin, daughter of Robert Wood,
without whose valuable assistance, love for her father,
and fantastic memory, this book could not have been written.

Table of Contents

Black and White Plates

Foreword

The Last Mountain, The Life of Robert Wood, is a refreshingly different art book, one that is surely welcome. It is an appealing and highly readable "portrait" of an artist, presented by an art lover who knew her subject chiefly as a creator at the canvas, which is what really matters.

This is a handsome and valuable addition to the Robert Wood legacy. Those who knew the artist and admired his works, and especially, those who did not, will find here an illuminating and loving study that captures the essence of the man and his art.

Glenn Tucker
Fine Arts Editor
San Antonio Light

Introduction

Writing this book has been a labor of love for me; almost as much labor as love, for I have never professed to being a writer. I am an art gallery owner, having started out as an artist.

The life of a gallery owner is exciting and rewarding. In addition to the hundreds of beautiful and significant paintings that pass through our doors each year, there are hundreds of interesting people. It is like basking in warm sunlight to hear the constant flow of appreciation of art which prevails; it is an atmosphere of harmony which is soul-satisfying.

In a single day I may have the privilege of helping a young couple select their very first painting, and also advise a collector on an investment in art. Then I may visit one or more artists. Some of my closest friends, in fact, are the artists I represent. My greatest, dearest, departed friend was Robert Wood, one of our nation's most creative artistic geniuses. In my fifteen years of gallery work, I have been asked to answer one question over and over again: "What is the artist like?" In this book I attempt to answer that question and many others about this truly great artist.

I have tried to paint a portrait of Robert Wood, who passed on before I could finish this book, a few days before his ninetieth birthday. He was a man who was as beautiful as the thousands of works that came from his inspired hands over a long and distinguished career.

I began corresponding with him in 1971, met him a few years later, visited him and his charming wife, Caryl, in California, and happily hosted him in my own home. His daughter, Florence Wood Brumaghin, I am happy to say, manages one of the Sigoloff Galleries in San Antonio.

Though I did not have the pleasure of meeting Robert Wood until very late in his life, I had already developed a profound admiration for his works over many years. I was struck both by the beauty and masterly technique of his paintings and by his unique philosophy of life.

Robert Wood never painted an unhappy picture. A child of

Robert Wood – 1976

nature, from his boyhood in England to his death in the shadow of a California mountain, he walked hand-in-hand with nature, and never ceased to marvel at her variety and infinite power. In every landscape and seascape, for nearly seventy years, he brought forth the love of God's handwork, whether his subject was a simple study of the Texas hill country or a majestic vision of the Pacific crashing to the shore at sunset.

This book also fulfills a promise made to the artist when he visited at my home. It was at that time that I asked him if I could write a book about his art and his life, and he, with that charming smile and twinkle in his eye, said, "Why, certainly. I would be honored."

I have tried to say something meaningful, not only about Robert Wood the artist, but about Robert Wood the man. There will, no doubt, be other books about him in the future, but none will be written out of greater love or admiration.

Violet Sigoloff Flume
San Antonio, Texas
Spring, 1982

The Last Mountain
The Life of Robert Wood

Part I

Reflection of the Artist at his Easel

How does an artist contemplate his final work? What does he think about, how does he focus his ideas on a theme that will, somehow, crystallize and epitomize his life's work? Does he seek for yet another discovery, continuing a lifelong quest for something new, another horizon? Or does he stay on the tried-and-true paths that have stood him in good stead all his life?

In Robert Wood's case, it was almost a combination of all these. True to his sympathies, he went to his constant source of inspiration, the one aspect of beauty that never failed to feed his spirit and his creative drive: Nature.

"Hmm," he mused, on a clear, cool day in February as he paced back and forth in his cluttered, familiar studio. "What shall I paint today?"

He faced the blank, eggshell-white canvas before him as he had done countless thousands of times. This time, he would not simply pick up his brush and go to work. This was a time for reflection.

Caryl had noted a slight change in his attitude and emotions over the past few days. He was even more serene, more composed and even quieter than normal. Always attentive to his wife and her comfort, he seemed even more so lately, always making sure to pull her chair out for her at the table, like the Old World gentleman as always, and was almost overly solicitous for her well-being. Did he know the end was near?

The canvas stood before him, barren, awaiting the master's touch again.

Robert walked to the window, took off his glasses and mused. And dreamed.

His mind may have wandered all the way back to Sandgate,

to the vision of a boy sitting high above the jagged cliffs overlooking the sea, sketch pad in hand and dreams of a faraway place in his head.

Perhaps he thought of Texas, too, and those years in San Antonio that were so good to him. Surely he thought of the Texas landscape: the gentle, rolling hills, the hot afternoons, the mesquite and live oak trees, the cool springs and rivers, the friendly people who brought him his first, measurable success.

He thought of his favorite subjects: the rolling sea against the rocks, the prairie at sunset, a staggering peak backdropping majestic trees, and the final image seized him.

"No matter how many mountains you climb in your life," Robert was fond of saying, "there is always one more facing you."

And so, Robert Wood sat down at his easel and began to sketch his farewell work, *The Last Mountain*.

This monumental painting, now in the custody of the Sigoloff Galleries in San Antonio, is like, and yet unlike, any other Robert Wood creation. The theme is a familiar one, of course, to the millions of Wood admirers: Mount Hood, one of the grandest peaks in the hemisphere and a standard mountain subject of the artist for many years.

And yet, there is a unique radiance pervading the painting, a level of spirituality and light found nowhere else in his work. The entire scene is bathed in light, a glowing, pure, intense whiteness that speaks of eternal things, of a scene set beyond time and space. The mountain emerges from this flood of radiance as a kind of symbol, a fixed point of destiny. In a way, it is a picture of all mountains rolled into one, the imaginary ones man must cross with his will, as well as the real ones he climbs with his body. In this final work, Robert Wood made his most permanent and enduring statement, summing up his philosophy of life and art in a single, dramatic landscape.

A few days later, complaining of breathing difficulties, he was admitted to the hospital in Bishop. There he died on March 15, 1979, just nine days before his ninetieth birthday.

Robert William Wood had climbed his last mountain.

Part II

The Early Years (1889-1924)

Sandgate is a perfect place for an artist to be born. A tiny friendly town on the Kentish Coast in Southern England, near the fabled White Cliffs of Dover, it is surrounded by scenic beauty, more than enough to stimulate the imagination of a young, creative temperament. The air is constantly bracing, full of salt spray tossed into the atmosphere from the strong Channel winds. Huge, forbidding rocks, molded into jagged giants from eons of wind and water, pose proudly against the sea, challenging always those who might come to shore and those who might sail away, in any season.

When rain and storm and gale are not whipping the rough, marshy grasses and the sun pushes through at midday, Sandgate is a scene that has inspired poets, composers, men of religion, and especially painters. Thick, billowing clouds move in majestic precision toward the tossing, restless ocean, their formations forming the shapes of mythical giants and beasts.

Spring comes and Nature is at its most ferocious. One can never conquer the elements here, and sensible people do not even try. Artists, however, glory in it – the vast and always changing land and seascapes – and they draw from it a never-ending inspiration.

At the peak of these violent wind-and-rain demonstrations by Nature, Robert William Wood, dean of American painters, was born at Sandgate on March 24, 1889, to his hard-working and artistic father, and his frail, sensitive wife, Annie Amelia.

The elder Wood, a struggling but much admired artist, operated a small hardware store in the town, and instilled early in

Victorian House in San Diego which the Woods restored.

Sandgate, England, his birthplace, as it is today.

With his dogs—1892

his sharp and sensitive son both an appreciation of beauty and the harsh realities of the world. At a time when most young boys are given balls or sticks to keep themselves amused, tiny Robert, at the tender age of four, was handed a pencil. His father would perch him on the curving rock wall that looks out over the turbulent promontory of rock and sea, and there, using discarded wrapping paper from the hardware store, the boy would spend hours sketching the billowing clouds against the startling blue of the sky, the waves lashing the coastline, and the ships. Those were his favorite subjects, for his mind was quickly susceptible to romance and fantasy. As incoming boats and ships appeared over the horizon or as outgoing ones vanished from his sight, he wondered and dreamed. Where are they coming from? Where are they going? What valuable cargoes lie secure in their holds? What far-off lands and people have they seen, what new wonders have they discovered? When he was a little older, he would wonder most of all about those boats heading across the Atlantic towards the New World. He did not know that one day he would make the journey himself, find success beyond his wildest dreams, and make it his home forever.

As the boy's interest and proficiency in drawing increased, his father began to recognize more than ordinary talent in his small offspring. When Robert wasn't busy shining shoes or polishing the myriad brass doorknobs on store fronts around Sandgate, he was busy sketching his landscapes and seascapes and the incoming and outgoing boats. When he reached the age of twelve, his father decided to find out whether anyone else could recognize the talent he found so obvious. It would be something of a financial sacrifice to send young Robert to art school in nearby Folkstone, for there were other mouths to feed: sisters, Dorothy, Ada and Hilda, and brothers Harry, Frank and Albert. (Another sister, Beatrice, died before Robert was born, and Harry died while still a youth). Later, when the great "Wood migration" to the United States occurred, the elder Wood arrived, his wife later, and they were followed by Hilda, Frank and Albert. The latter, who was called "Bert," achieved

June – 1901

some success as an artist himself on the west coast. Dorothy and Ada remained in England.

At Folkstone School, Robert's talent blossomed into spectacular achievements. Over the next seven years he won four first prizes and three second prizes in annual competitions at the academy, a record achievement for one of the school's students. Painting vigorously, the teenage Robert Wood gave full promise of the prolific artistic output that was to characterize his entire career.

At the school and during this training period Robert drew and painted myriad variations of the themes that had first caught his imagination at the age of four: the waves crashing to the shore, the ships with their exotic destinies and the stormy skies of southern England. These themes, in fact, underscored his work during his entire lifetime. When living in Bishop, California, at the close of his career, one of his favorite pastimes was floating tiny boats on the pond behind his home – an activity that was a passion of his boyhood days.

And his passion for storms and violent weather stood with him to his dying day. His daughter, Florence Wood Brumaghin, says that all his life Robert Wood loved to walk and think in violent rainy weather. Unafraid and stimulated by the crescendoes of lightning, thunder and sheets of rain, the artist found in these eternal forces of Nature his whole reason for being. And even though the major body of his work centered on serene, brilliantly colored pastoral scenes, whether the majestic mountains and valleys of the American West, or shore and coastline vistas of the Pacific, Robert Wood never failed to convey the raw, yet beautiful power that lies beneath the surface, as realized by Nature. He was, by his own admission, "Always conscious of God's handiwork in the world I see around me."

Having seen God's handiwork on the sometimes warm, sometimes wild Kentish Coast, Robert Wood, on reaching his young manhood, decided to spread his wings and search out the hand of Nature and Fate on foreign shores. For better or worse, he resolved to find himself and extend the reaches of his work in America.

Military picture and postcard written to his mother 1909

The year was 1910. The Statue of Liberty beckoned with particular emphasis this year and a flood of European immigrants arrived at Ellis Island and other East Coast stations as masses of humanity, some oppressed, some persecuted, and some, like twenty-one-year-old Robert Wood, were filled with wanderlust and unbridled confidence in their own abilities. Although his father, mother, brothers and sisters would join him in the New World, Robert was the first to arrive, accompanied by a close friend and confidant, Claude Waters. The artist had scraped and saved twenty-five pounds (about $160 in today's currency) but had stored years of faith in his talents. With enthusiasm and grit, he set out to explore his unfamiliar surroundings.

It seems odd, but the wiry, enthusiastic young Englishman's first real taste of American work was as a farm hand! Claude Waters' uncle owned a rugged section of farmland in Big Rock, Illinois, not far from Chicago, and it was here that the young men found themselves soon after disembarking at New York. The work was hard and the days were long, as the boys were up before dawn to milk the cows, perform a variety of other barnyard chores, then drive the milk by wagon to the village. The weather often was frightful – below zero some mornings – and the icy winds chilled them to the bone. Robert said later he did not mind the rigors of the farm because he was so happy, at last, to be in America.

But success was not ready to reach out its hand to the wide-eyed young painter immediately. Robert Wood soon learned that life was rough, if not rougher, in America than it was in England. Art was a rather new-fangled notion in the country that was just little more than a century old. Art works for the most part were considered the province of the wealthy, and fees that would allow an artist to earn a living were reserved only for the precious few.

As a result, Robert was forced to become a jack-of-all-trades, earning his daily bread by his wits wherever he could and however he could. Traveling mostly by hopping freight cars – often riding atop the huge machines with sketch pad in hand to record the varied and ever-changing countryside – he would stop wherever the trains stopped. Whether the destination was a large city or rustic village, the artist would "set up camp" with his meager provisions, dash off miniature sketches and drawings which he sold for only pocket change, or he would earn a small day's pay by painting signs òr helping in whatever odd jobs he could find.

But Robert Wood had the kind of temperament to survive the rigor of such a hand-to-mouth existence. In fact, he relished it and gloried in it. Free as the birds he saw sailing overhead during his sojourns across the broad landscape of America, and without any attachments to bind him to responsibility, he played the role of a latter-day Johnny Appleseed, dispensing art as the folk hero scattered seeds. As if to prove his detachment and disinterest in worldly possessions, he once tossed all his belongings bound up in a knapsack, off a boxcar, leaving him only with the clothes on his back.

Two years of wandering, looking and absorbing, found him in the sunny climes of Florida, and there, for the first time in his life though by no means the last, Robert fell in love.

He met a fifteen-year-old beauty named Eyssel Del Wagoner, and it is safe to say they stole each other's hearts. In that year (1912) it was not unusual for girls of fifteen to make a marriage, and many men by the time they were twenty-three already were married. The young beauty, whose reddish gold hair picked up and radiated highlights from the sun, was completely smitten by this dashing intense young Englishman with his tales of travel and the worlds he was going to conquer. She wanted to share in these colorful and far-flung adventures, so the two were married in Jacksonville, another city by the sea.

Soon restlessness got the better of young Robert. With his young bride in tow, he ventured north again, aiming his sights this time on the Midwest and the fertile Ohio Valley. They came to settle in St. Johns, Ohio, a pretty river town with immense tall trees, rolling farmland and gentle hills. It looked like the Cotswolds of England and then, at least for awhile, Robert felt at home.

Five days before Christmas in 1913, Robert Wood's respon-

1915

sibilities took on a major addition with the birth of a daughter, Florence Adeline, whom he and nearly everyone later would call "Kitty".

Kitty was a smiling, adoring, precocious child, eager to please her parents, and quick to assume her duties in the small, restless household.

"Even though I was the apple of his eye," she says today, "my father really and truly wanted a son. So I tried my best to be like a boy in a lot of ways. My father, who had been quite a boxer in his youth in England, taught me how to box and it certainly came in handy. Once, when I was about four, I received a beautiful, delicately painted miniature ivory fan from my aunt Dorothy in England. It would open and close and had been fashioned into a beautiful necklace. It became one of my favorite possessions. One day, two older neighborhood boys of about six snatched the necklace and tried to run away with it. I got into a fight with them and promptly gave each of them a black eye. Later, the parents came to our house to complain about their sons being beaten up, but they changed their tune when they learned that a four-year-old girl had done the deed. My father got a big kick out of that. He was proud of me in many ways. He was a firm disciplinarian at home, always making sure I did well at school, but he was always a loving and tender man.

"My fondest early memories are of my father and mother, ever the young lovers, strolling hand-in-hand through the woods or by a stream, and my father pointing out all the beauties – hidden and revealed – wherever we walked. He liked to call the sunrise 'God's smile.' And he would talk to me about seeing the reality of the world around me. 'If people would only stop and look!' he would say. 'Most people don't take time to see God's work. It's there, in the ocean, in the mountains, in all living things, and in the colors all around us!' He was wonderful."

Robert Wood was quick to put a pencil in his four-year-old daughter's hand, just as his father had done for him, but it appeared that young Kitty's talents were going to lie elsewhere: cooking, and music lessons which were paid for by the artist's paintings. These works were not selling with any regularity at the time, but provided at least a modest income for the struggling young painter and his family. (Later, a dealer would buy out Robert Wood's entire collection to launch him on his fabulous career, from which he never looked back, nor had to.)

The challenging frontier of the Great Northwest was the next lure for the artist. He took his young family to Seattle, Washington, where Robert's father, William, joined them.

"I loved my grandfather," Kitty says. "He was forever shopping with me and buying me pretty things. Whenever I was invited to birthday parties, he would buy the gift for my friend, and he would also buy an identical item for me."

But there was tragedy in the wind as well. Robert Wood's mother, a tiny wisp of a woman, had understood that in America no liquor was for sale and this was the best news she could have hoped for, because her husband had a lifelong problem with drink.

"She was cheerful and lively," according to Kitty, "just like a little bird when she first came to America. When the problem with alcohol was still present with my grandfather, she literally died of a broken heart. She just went to sleep one night and never awakened."

The elder Wood and his son parted company in California shortly after the painter's mother's death. But mostly, the Seattle period was a happy time: Robert got his much-awaited son, John Robert, who was called "Buster" (born June 20, 1919), and it was a close-knit, happy family. One of Kitty's most vivid memories from those years is of her father, an accomplished musician himself, playing the mandolin – in the house and by the campfire on their frequent trips to see the wonders of nature. Eyssel played the ukelele and all would sing, mostly in the evenings. It was about this time, too, that Robert painted one of his rare portraits, using his still teen-aged bride as the subject. The painting ended up in Chicago, in the home of Kitty's maternal grandmother, and she has not seen it since she was seventeen.

What a fortune this painting, if located today, would bring! It is doubtful that the artist signed it – later in the 1920's, he would paint many oils without signing his name, and often adopted a pseudonym. Also while Robert Wood became the most "reproduced" artist of all time, surpassing even the Old Masters, it is believed that no prints have been made of his extremely rare portrait work.

A subject of great concern to the artist was the health of his tender young son. His frail condition sent the family hopscotching across the country again, with the hope to find a more suitable climate: California, Oregon, Missouri, Kansas and many points between.

Kitty Wood recalls the journeys, giving some remarkable pictures of her father's strength of character, his sense of humor, his playfulness, his fearless demeanor and his artistic temperament.

"We traveled for about a year trying to find a location that would suit my brother's health. We started from Washington State. I remember my father bought a police dog which he named Prince; he was a descendant of Strong Heart, the famous movie dog of silent films. We hadn't traveled far across the Washington prairie when we stopped to let the dog out. He headed right back across the prairie as fast as he could go. My father said, as Prince went out of sight: 'Well, he's gone.' We stayed there for awhile, but all of a sudden we saw a tiny speck coming our way. My tears stopped as I saw it was our beautiful dog racing back toward us. He never ran away again.

"In those days, there were no super highways or large towns. We had a touring car with our grub box and camping equipment on the running board of our car, plus the trunk. It was the duty of my brother and me to blow up the rubber mat every night. I was about ten; my brother five. Whenever we saw a likely town, we would stop in a campground for a few weeks and my father would paint his pictures and sell them. I remember a scary scene once when we were in Oregon. We came around a curve with a big patch of ice on it. Two or three cars had already skidded around the curve and went over a tremendous cliff. There weren't any guard rails. My father told my mother to get out of the car and take my brother and me and then walk down, because it was so unsafe. My mother refused, telling him, "Bob, if you go over, we all go." So, Daddy started down the mountain. The car skidded sideways, and that is the way we went down; just a hair's breadth from the edge of a 1,000-foot drop. My mother said she was never once afraid; she had all the confidence in the world in him.

"As we traveled across country, my father trained Prince to jump. He could get him to leap about seven feet high. He even taught him to play hide-and-seek. We would all hide, and Prince would find us; then he would hide and we would hunt him. At night my father would build a campfire. We were in a wilderness and would sit around the fire; my father played the mandolin and my mother the ukelele, and we would all sing. It sounded so lovely. The coyotes would howl and Prince would answer them back. Those were lovely years."

The Woods, after a brief stopover in Excelsior Springs, Missouri, made a stop of a few months in Garden City, Kansas.

"It was a nice little town as I remember," recalls Kitty Wood. "My daddy set up his easel and started painting. My brother, some other children and I were playing in an old abandoned schoolhouse, until all at once we saw the largest snake we had ever seen. I screamed and people came running from everywhere — even the town sheriff. Daddy searched all around, found the snake, then let out a big laugh. He said it was just a harmless garden snake, then he caught it and held its head above his own, while its tail dragged the ground. My father wasn't afraid of anything.

"Our first experience in California was fun. We stopped along the road where olive orchards were. We all loved the beautiful scenery, which my father remarked on more than once, though he never realized at the time that California would be his final home. We stopped at a little place called Rose Bend and went swimming. Mother pretended she was drowning, and Prince jumped in the water and swam out to her, dragging her to shore. Of course the dog thought he had done something wonderful, and my father praised him lavishly.

"We had quite an experience coming across the California

desert. The only road was made of simple wooden boards, just wide enough to accommodate one car. If you met a car, whichever one got to a little platform first pulled in and waited. I think we met one car, and it took all day to cross the desert. But then, there was no vegetation at all – just the beautiful sand dunes always changing shapes and sizes with the wind.

"My father made our ice box by lining it with gunny sacks, making a hole, then putting a cover on it. Our milk, butter, and eggs stayed fresh.

"Daddy and I used to go for long walks together, even after he and mother were divorced (1925). He would point out the beauties of Nature, things I never would think to look for, and now, after more than fifty years, I still look at the delicate shape of a tree, the tilt of a bird's head, the beautiful sights of silken oats swaying in the wind, the majestic, tall trees, the beautiful ripple of a stream, the sun making shadows and light patterns as we walked through the forest, and, of course, 'God's smile.' My father taught me how to swim. I had always been a little afraid of the water, but he told me to put my head under, open my eyes and just look around. I did, and I was amazed at what I could see. Never again was I afraid of water."

The collapse of the Wood marriage was a traumatic experience for all concerned. Kitty feels that one of the major stumbling blocks was her father's passion for neatness and cleanliness, especially around the house.

"My father was a very neat person and didn't allow things to be cluttered," Kitty says. "Eyssel was not a very neat person as a housekeeper."

Once, in fact, Kitty, when a little girl, had left her pencil on the floor. She saw her father coming toward her, apparently to reprimand her; so she scooped up the pencil and put it behind her back just as Robert took a smack at her posterior. The pencil point went into his hand, the lead becoming embedded in his thumb. The scar remained with him until his death.

"We lived in Portland, Oregon, for awhile. We used to go to Seaside, a summer resort, because a friend owned a summer house there. It had a music room with piano and drums set up.

My father taught me how to play the drums then.

"Sometimes my father, when he was in a playful mood, dressed up in an old, striped bathing suit, derby, cane and monocle. Someone took a photograph of him in this outlandish get-up, and when mother saw the picture, she captioned it, 'Lord, Help Us!'

"A little later, we were on the beach when a small plane passed overhead and upside down. Mother said that anyone foolish enough to do that had to be crazy. When daddy came in for lunch she told him about it, and with a twinkle in his eye, he casually told her that it was he who had been the passenger in the plane. Nothing, absolutely nothing, frightened him."

Oregon – which before 1925 was largely dominated by wilderness and thick forest – was sort of a "gypsy camp" for the young Wood family in the critical years of 1919-1923, and certainly it suited the artistic temperament of the eternal vagabond, Robert Wood.

Claude Waters, the friend with whom he sailed from England, homesteaded there, staking out a large plot of land in the forest, and often arrived with horse and buggy (cars were not seen in those parts then) to pick up Robert, Eyssel and the young Kitty, to bring them back with him for a visit. Robert recalled that Claude "had a fireplace large enough to put a small tree in," and Kitty said the fireplace took up the width of the rustic house.

Kitty loved to sit on a tiny, curving seat in the corner near the huge, pot-bellied stove Claude used to heat his cabin. It was close to a small room where Claude kept his apple cider, and Kitty recalls many happy nights in which the quartet would drink the sweet cider and enjoy impromptu musicals, with her father banging away on his mandolin, Claude picking his guitar, Eyssel and Kitty singing. Robert, forever the clown, would keep the group in stitches with his antics whenever the music stopped. If he had not become an artist, Robert Wood probably could have made a good living as a vaudeville comedian.

The Northwest experience proved, after a time to be a dead-end street for Robert, so he decided to pull up stakes with his young eager family and strike out for new territory. His wanderings took him on a jigsaw pattern across the country; but ever moving east and south, he found the land that he would make his home for many years and which would prove unusually fruitful for his career: Texas.

Part III

The Texas Years (1924-1941)

When Robert Wood moved to Texas in 1924, after his vagabond meanderings across the country, he came to a state that
had not begun to realize its potential. San Antonio, with a
population of nearly 300,000 at the time, was the state's largest
city, but Dallas and Houston were gaining fast, the latter from
its burgeoning oil resources and proximity to the Gulf of Mexico.

Robert probably chose the San Antonio area for several
reasons. The city's location was perfect, with the coast a scant
150 miles away; abundant hills and ranches just outside the city
limits to the north, and the windswept flatlands to the west;
more than enough scenic riches to appeal to an artist.

But the city was something more. It had a relaxed, leisurely-
paced lifestyle (it still does), splendid weather, and most endear-
ing of all, it had the state's richest art colony. The hundreds
of charming adobe homes, resplendent Victorian and Georgian
mansions, a lazy river that wound through the heart of the
downtown area, and whose banks were dotted with artists at
their easels throughout the year, served as a great stimulus to
the impressionable young Englishman. Robert throughout his
life often said he felt "right at home" the first time he discovered
San Antonio. He was thirty-five at the time and he made the
area his home for seventeen years.

Many friends and fellow artists who knew him through his
career recalled Robert often referring to San Antonio as "my
second home." He conducted a love affair with the city that was
to hold him all his life. He liked nothing better than spending
a day beside the downtown river, or walking on the grounds

of the old Spanish Missions, or visiting the hill country, or setting up his easel by a roadside dotted with bluebonnets. Indeed, Texas in general and San Antonio in particular never stopped being a source of inspiration for the canvases of Robert Wood. His brushes and oils sang eloquent praises to the historical monuments that were everywhere; the coast, the desert areas, the hills, for more than half a century. Often in his writings and conversation, the artist affirmed that no state offered the scenic variety as did Texas, a sentiment that has been echoed many times by other artists.

San Antonio has remained a thriving art center, and Robert Wood's settling there for seventeen years is one of the reasons it has stayed so. From his prodigious output during the years 1924-1941, his teaching and his encouragement of other artists, along with his commanding and forceful personality, San Antonio can rank him still as one of its most illustrious and important artistic residents, whose influence is still being felt.

Before settling in San Antonio, however, Robert Wood and his family kept up their customary gypsy existence by "scouting the territory" first. They tried life in several small towns in South Texas and the Gulf Coast, staying the longest in Corpus Christi, where the artist went back to the formula that worked for him so well in the Great Northwest – setting up his easel in store windows and dashing off his "buckeye" paintings for the fascinated gawkers on the street. He became such a "draw" that the Corpus Christi newspaper sent a reporter to do a story on the lightning-fast artist who was dashing off finished pictures in just minutes. The paper devoted almost a full column to the dashing Englishman's slapdash paintings. From the sales of these works, Robert was able to take his family to San Antonio and stay long enough to decide that this was where he wanted to live.

He was certainly right in his hunch about the city. From San Antonio, Robert Wood finally gained the regional and national attention that his art deserved. Almost from the time he took up residence in San Antonio, in the old Los Angeles Heights section of the city, he made a lasting impact on the town's artistic climate. His works started to sell, he was beginning to be noticed by knowledgeable buyers and collectors, and he was able at last to support his family in a style that allowed him to pursue his career without worry.

The family lived in an old, but elegant, two-storied house that would eventually be turned into a small art colony itself. During the day, Robert labored in a studio he opened downtown – now the site of a popular Mexican restaurant catering mostly to tourists – and worked modestly in a nearby paint store, whose owners cleared a section to make some gallery space available for the artist. Robert had no trouble keeping the walls of the makeshift gallery full with his Texas landscapes, seascapes and hill country scenes. Always a prolific painter – a few years before he accomplished the phenomenal feat of fifty oil paintings in a single day for a commission – he would have fresh oils available as soon as the walls were cleared of his works.

The young Kitty often would be called in to "manage" the gallery while her father went on one of his frequent painting "tours," which happened whenever the traveling "bug" bit him.

"These 'tours' were really just an excuse my father used to get out of town for awhile," recalls his daughter. "Robert Wood often would accompany a jewelry salesman to the various towns and cities in south and central Texas on his route. At each location, and whenever possible, my father would whip out his easel, and finish a picture on the spot. Quite often he sold the painting right then and there."

After many years, Kitty is still in the art gallery managing business, as she is today the manager for one of the Sigoloff Galleries in San Antonio.

The paint store gallery served as a springboard for Robert Wood's emergence as a major talent in Texas art circles. Other stores in San Antonio began sending buyers to the tiny shop to purchase Wood paintings for their own business places. Robert found himself having to work with almost assembly-line precision to keep his buyers supplied, but the income he derived from the sales was not sensational. At the time, the oil paintings were selling for twenty dollars or less.

It was another artist – A.D. Greer – who brought Robert Wood increased financial remuneration for his works although, he laughs today, at his own expense.

A.D. Greer, who has spent a lifetime painting the Texas scene and who admits to heavy influence of Robert Wood, recalled: "I found out how little Robert was making on his paintings, and I approached Arthur Sierwaersky, who owned a publishing company and who was an enthusiastic art dealer. He had become very impressed with Robert Wood's paintings at the paint store gallery, and when I told him that R.W. was 'available,' he wanted me to set up a meeting with the artist as soon as possible. We met in a sample showroom which was maintained by the St. Anthony hotel, and R.W. told Arthur that he was getting forty dollars per painting which, of course, was about twice the figure he was actually getting. Arthur didn't blink an eye. He said 'Fine' and immediately started buying all of Robert Wood's work he could get his hands on. That blew me out of the tub, because he didn't want my paintings any more."

Two events of historic importance grew out of the modest little downtown gallery: Robert Wood met Jose Arpa, one of the two or three top painters in the state at the time, and an outstanding teacher; and a young, teenage boy named Porfirio Salinas.

Arpa became a close and deeply personal friend of Robert Wood in the mid-1920's, and Arpa became the only formal teacher that Robert ever had in the United States. It was Arpa who pointed out the inherent beauties of San Antonio's colorful old missions, then in a state of semi-ruin. The two often took easels, brushes and oils to Espada, San Jose and Concepcion, to spend a day in conversation and professional execution with their brushes. Arpa at once recognized Robert Wood's genius and creative talent. The San Antonio Express noted: "There is a new star on the art horizon in our city. His name is Robert Wood, and San Antonians are now vying heatedly for his latest works."

The fourteen-year-old Porfirio Salinas, who in later years would become known as Texas' foremost bluebonnet painter and the favorite artist of the late President Lyndon B. Johnson, walked into the paint store gallery one morning and asked Robert Wood for a job. Wood tried to dismiss the shining-faced youngster, but was impressed with his directness and attitude. After thinking a few minutes, the artist told the boy he would give him a part-time job as a floor sweeper. The young Salinas readily accepted, and that simple decision led to Porfirio Salinas' long and illustrious career in art.

Robert recognized that Porfirio Salinas was no ordinary young man when one day he noticed the boy sketching on cigar box lids. Recognizing talent, Robert began giving the youngster lessons in painting and soon the gentle landscapes of the younger artist were attracting a great deal of attention, too, a fact which pleased Robert immensely. Above all, Robert Wood admired the delicate brush strokes of the young student, and many years later was heard to say: "I never met an artist who had a softer touch than Salinas."

In just little over a year after making San Antonio their home, in mid-1925, the Woods were divorced. It was a painful experience for all, with the young and still beautiful Eyssel going off to Chicago to live with her mother, and the children remaining with their father. Later, Eyssel remarried and she and Robert were never to see each other again.

Kitty, just fourteen, was placed in the senior class at the old Los Angeles Heights High School (it no longer exists) because of the academic excellence of her previous schooling.

Robert, cast now in the role of both mother and father, took on the task with his customary zeal. He was a loving but strict parent to Kitty and Buster, and although he provided for them in every way, he did not coddle or indulge them extravagantly. Buster was enrolled in the city's famous Peacock Military Academy, while Kitty was given private music lessons in piano and violin.

Kitty became her father's principal aide and helper. In addition to music, he saw that she knew how to ride a horse, swim, defend herself, and especially how to run a kitchen.

"My father paid for my music lessons with his beautiful paintings," Kitty recalled. "My piano teacher, Mary Brendell, still cherishes the works she received for providing lessons. I took violin lessons for awhile, too, and my string teacher, Leona Rahm, also prized the oil paintings she received. In high school I went in for a lot of sports, and my father, who was very athletic himself, trained me for many of the county tournaments and competitions in which I was entered."

But Kitty soon saw that cooking was to be her true artistic expression, and her father was quick to point out the similarities between chef and artist.

"A cook," he told her "can be likened to a painter. An artist has a teacher who directs him in the mixing and application of paint to the canvas. The student must then use his own initiative to create his own picture. The same is true of a cook. I can give you the basic ingredients, but you must create the many varied, delicious dishes. You will find that you can create with food just as easily as an artist creates with paint."

It is a lesson she never forgot, and to please her father, Kitty often prepared some dishes that were popular in England but virtually unknown in America: "Shrimp Wiggle," which is prepared with shrimp and cream sauce and served with English peas on toast; steak and kidney pie, roast beef with Yorkshire pudding, and many others. Robert never failed to compliment his daughter gallantly whenever he felt she had done well in the kitchen.

Another valuable lesson Kitty learned from her father was an appreciation of the dignity of work, no matter how menial it seemed to be.

"If you're going to do something, do it right!" was her father's frequent advice to his daughter (and to his art students). "No matter what kind of job you have, if it is honest work, then go ahead with it and do your best at it."

Over the years, after Kitty married and her father moved permanently to California, she would treasure the words of wisdom from her father, who never ceased to communicate his thoughts and good advice to her. She saved every letter her father wrote to her, even the ones written to her during her teenage years.

In this Texas period of Robert Wood's career – the late 1920's and 30's – the artist adopted a rather unique way of identifying himself with his paintings. During this decade of prodigious output, Robert adopted several pseudonyms when he signed his canvases "G. Day," "Trebor" (Robert spelled in reverse), and "R. Wood." Those canvases he felt did not come up to his standards, he did not sign at all. Later in his career, when he was given the opportunity to examine some of these earlier works, he added his customary signature "Robert Wood" to those he felt deserved to be signed. There are still a number of paintings signed "G. Day," particularly in the Texas market where most of them originated. When he left Texas, and to the end of his career, he signed his works simply "Robert Wood."

Following his divorce, Robert certainly did not abandon his admiration for women. Although he would deny that he was a "ladies' man," his artistic temperament and steel-blue eyes proved irresistible to many women during his long and colorful career. In San Antonio he began to date a talented artist, Alice Chilton, who introduced him to the Christian Science Church. Robert never formally identified himself with any organized church, but his daughter maintains that he was always "a very spiritually minded man who lived his religion in day to day appreciation of God's bountiful blessings." She says: "It made itself known most often when he and I walked together in the woods or beside a stream or river. He never failed to point out the beauties of Nature and the need to appreciate the scenic beauty as it was in realty."

Robert seemed at times to be flirting with the idea of becoming a showman of sorts, and often put his vaudeville-like talents to work in his early San Antonio days. Vaudeville, of course, was very big in those days – the top names in show business, such as Jack Benny and George Burns, played the national circuit, which included San Antonio. There was a popular stage act, designed to entertain the audience while the stars changed costumes, in which an artist or a group of artists completed a painting before one's eyes while an organ or orchestra played some stirring tune of the day. Naturally, Robert, the born performer, had to try his hand at this, too.

On the stage of the newly built Majestic Theatre, one of the most magnificent theatre structures in the world, Robert proved such a hit with the audience as he dashed off a seascape to an orchestral accompaniment that he stepped over his allotted time. The star backstage was fuming at being upstaged by such an unknown that he almost refused to go on. As the orchestra played on, Robert reproduced a seascape, a mountain scene or a landscape with true oil paint on a genuine canvas in less than seven minutes. No wonder the star was annoyed!

Interesting to note is that the beautiful Majestic Theatre has recently been restored and is again showing the current plays and headliners of today.

In 1932 the Wood family moved outside the San Antonio City limits to "the country" – off the famous Scenic Loop Road near the community of Helotes, now a highly prized and expensive real estate development. It was called then the Scenic Loop Playground, but in reality it was a sixty-home development with two spring-fed swimming pools and miles of wide open spaces; just the sort of environment where Robert Wood could work in the middle of Nature, which is always where he preferred to be.

Robert's "country estate," more fitting to his new-found status as a successful artist, was a rustic rock house to which he added a studio, partitioned it off from the main structure and spent most of each day, seven days a week.

Robert was the perfect "country host," welcoming all who would stop by and never failing to serve tea to his afternoon callers, especially the women of the area, whom he treated with customary gallantry and charm. (A popular story at the time was that, whenever a man arrived home and found his wife missing, he would be told: "Oh, she's probably having tea with Robert.")

The dashing Robert, almost as much athlete as artist, was an avid swimmer – he became expert at it in his boyhood days on the English coast; but, being of a Bohemian nature, wasn't particular about what he wore when he dived in. At that time,

With his daughter Florence at Scenic Loop in Texas—
1935

men's swimsuits had coverings for the chest as well as the lower extremities, but Robert disdained such attire, plunging into the cold waters wearing only a pair of shorts. Several of the more conservative neighbors looked rather askance at such immodest apparel, but the artist's charming, gracious ways earned him an easy forgiveness and tolerance. He was, in fact, among the first to be invited to the myriad house parties and social gatherings of the growing little community, and needless to say, always proved to be the life of the party with his ready wit, jokes and improvised song-and-dance routines.

There were nearly always parties of some sort on weekends in the summer, as many San Antonians maintained "weekend" retreats in the area, escaping to them on Friday afternoons, returning Sundays and throwing parties in the interim.

In addition to swimming and other athletic pursuits, Robert also loved to hike and climb the many hills around Scenic Loop. One he found particularly treacherous, and he promptly nicknamed it "The Bucket of Blood Hill."

While the Woods were living in the country setting of Scenic Loop, most of his works were being sought by a prosperous couple, George and Rachel Allen, who owned a store where the works were offered for sale. There were days of excitement, too as Robert, with a friend, Ollie Wetstone, had the chance to play real-life heroes by saving a drowning woman.

The two men were basking in the sun by one of the chilly, spring-fed pools when they heard cries for help. A pretty young woman apparently found herself in water that was far over her head and began to sink, swallowing water, and terrified. Hearing her cries and ever ready to rescue a damsel in distress, Robert, fully clothed, dived into the frigid water, pulled her to the surface, then expertly swam to the shore with her in his arms.

When she had recovered some composure, she asked, tearfully: "How can I ever thank you?" Robert's laconic reply was, "You can dry my pants."

Says his daughter: "He never ceased to amaze and delight me. Once he decided to take me fishing near the house where we lived. For the fun of it, he put a little perch on the end of a fishing line while I wasn't looking, and tugged gently on the pole to give me the thrill of catching a fish. Imagine his surprise, and mine, when I pulled the pole out of the water and discovered that I had caught a much larger fish that had swallowed the small one my father had put on the line."

One of the reasons Robert endeared himself to his neighbors was his habit of giving small paintings as tokens of appreciation, or for anniversaries and birthdays.

Of all the women Robert met and courted during the period shortly after his divorce from Eyssel, two are worthy of special mention: Alice Chilton, a blonde, delicate beauty who was one of Robert's students and a talented painter in her own right; and Tula Murphy, whom he subsequently married.

Alice Chilton dated Robert for several years and truly loved him. When he met Tula and jilted Alice, she was crushed and heartbroken. (She subsequently married a singer, Gilbert Ware, and died in San Antonio in the early 1970's).

Tula Murphy must have been a ravishing creature, for she turned the woman-wise head of Robert Wood completely. She caused strong likes and dislikes among her contemporaries, several of whom I was able to interview during the course of collecting material for this book. Depending on their point of view, they described Tula alternately as "attractive but not beautiful," "small but aggressive," "very possessive," "vivacious, effusive, flowery, sweet," and "mean."

Gifted in literature she wrote poetry and gracious, charming letters. When Robert took his new bride to visit one of his neighbors in the early 1930's, they noticed the house was decorated in a profusion of bright colors, to which Tula responded: "I just vibrate to these colors."

The years rolled by with Robert Wood gaining in stature among his peers and taking his place among the handful of Texas' most honored artists. His works gained in acceptance rapidly, and he was able to command higher prices for his works with each passing year. But it was a time of heartache for him, too. One day his son, Buster, left home and never returned to

At work on portrait – 1936

his father's house again. In fact, Robert and his son barely communicated after the departure, and evidently he was sorely disappointed in his son. (Buster died in 1969).

His daughter, meanwhile, matured into a beauty and soon her hand was claimed in marriage in 1937. At the age of twenty-three she married Edward Beran, the ceremony being conducted in the Wood home in the country with a reception at a famous restaurant in the woodlands, the Grey Moss Inn, which still today is a thriving, well-known inn. Edward's company transferred him to Texarkana, in East Texas, shortly after the marriage. A son, William, always thereafter called Billy, was born in November, 1939. When the infant boy was six months old, the family moved back to the San Antonio area, which delighted Robert, for his grandson was one of the joys of his life.

"My father visited us often when we moved back," Kitty recalls. "He got a great kick out of romping and playing with Billy, and their love for each other was mutual. Billy always thought of his grandfather as someone special, and vice versa. My father all his life was a great lover of children, but since Billy was of his own flesh and blood, he gave him special, loving attention."

Through the years Robert's pride in Billy was always apparent, and the two maintained a close relationship always. Perhaps Billy filled many of the gaps left by his son. Billy still remains in San Antonio and his wife, Nancy, just presented him with a baby girl, Robert Wood's first and only great grandchild.

The Texas years were the "proving ground" for Robert Wood and his art, and during this critical period of his career his deft and unmistakable style of artistic expression was perfected. For boldness of conception and finesse of execution, Robert Wood almost stands alone among American artists, and it was his Texas period that underscored his technical wizardry and mastery of the landscape and seascape canvas. Warm, glowing colors were his trademark in those years, with a delicate, refined subtlety of development in line and almost musical virtuosity in his brush strokes. His works from this period showed an extraordinary juxtaposition of massive forms and sen-

Sketching in field of wildflowers, Texas – 1940

sitive lines and these concepts remained the hallmark of his works, even those he painted to his final days on earth.

With the outbreak of World War II in 1939 and with the entry of the United States into the conflict shortly thereafter, Robert was nudged again by the gypsy traveling fever. He decided to pull up roots again; a remarkable decision considering the artist was, at this time, fifty-two years old and at the peak of his powers creatively. His reputation was already at its height in Texas and the Southwest, and he had gained a national following, so it would seem that he would have been wise to remain in San Antonio and continue to add to his artistic stature.

But it was not to be. Looking west, Robert decided to move and reach for a new territory for his canvases. Because of its abundance of beauty – mountains, sea, sand – and its generally delightful climate, the artist chose California, the Golden State. He was to make California his final home (even though he made several more moves within the state's boundaries) and from here he would achieve international acclaim and power. The trial years were over, and Robert Wood was now ready to stake his claim, not in forgotten gold mines or forbidding mountains, where many men had lost their fortunes and even their lives, but in the varied landscape of what is now our most populous state, and he would make an indelible impression, not only upon himself and the art colony in which he would become virtually a king, but on the art-buying public as well.

The number of prominent artists who have confessed to a profound influence by Robert Wood is inestimable, but it is safe to say that there is hardly a realistic painter working in the United States today who is not aware of Robert Wood's shadow, which now after his death, will loom larger and larger over the artistic landscape as the years roll on.

Part IV

The California Years (1941-1979)

California, "the land of orange blossoms and sunshine" had changed prodigiously since Robert Wood last saw it in the middle 1920's. It was growing at an unbelievable pace, property had gone up enormously in price, and times were hard, although the artist and Tula were enjoying relative prosperity when they pulled up their Texas roots in 1941 and decided to stake their claim on the west coast.

It was a difficult time for people to be making a new home. The United States was joining its Allies in Europe to fight Hitler's Germany; the whole country was at work and nearly everyone's energy was focused on the war effort. But not Robert Wood. An English citizen (he never became an American citizen, preferring to call himself "a friendly alien") who cared only for painting, he chose to spread his personal gospel of beauty from another vantage point.

He first chose the rugged, scenic upper coast near Carmel and the Monterey Peninsula as his new base of operations, for he became fascinated by the majestic mountains, the gnarled windswept cypress trees that jutted from the forbidding cliffs, and the fierce, stormy crash of the Pacific. Some of Robert Wood's most memorable seascapes emerged from this period. He turned out hundreds of breathtaking studies of the ocean, the endless variety of the coastline, the mountain ranges near the area, particularly the Grand Tetons, and sunsets on the restless water. These tremendous and famous works from this period have been reproduced thousands of times on posters and calendars and are among the most valuable in the entire Wood

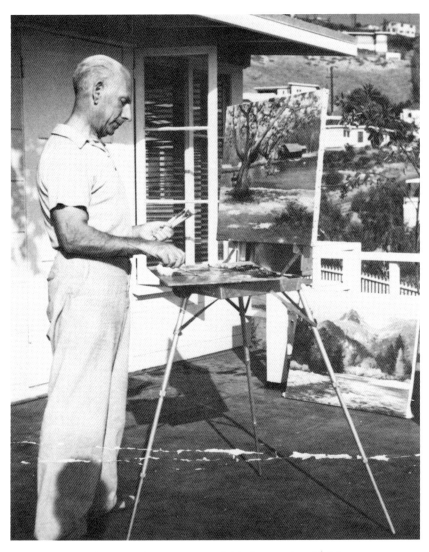

At Easel on patio of his home in Calif.

body of work. They are also appropriately difficult to find and afford.

Robert and Tula stayed seven years in California, mostly around Laguna Beach, and more out of his restless, gypsy nature than from boredom, the artist decided to try his hand at painting in the East again, another location he had not seen for many years.

Woodstock, New York, which has long been a colony for artists, most notably watercolorists, was recommended to Robert and he found a quaint, attractive, Walden-like studio in the woods. He made friends quickly and easily in his new environment, as he never failed to do, and among his closest artistic allies was Anton Fisher, then doing cover illustrations for The Saturday Evening Post.

Upstate New York proved as varied and challenging a landscape as the Pacific Coast had been, so Robert was out practically every morning with his famous sketch pad. One of his favorite subjects was the glorious fall coloring of the maples and elms around his studio, and many winter scenes with snow piled deep around the forest and cold, sparkling moonlight illuminating his mind and inspiration.

It was at this time, the late 1940's, that Robert created his famous "Four Season" landscapes that have become so immensely popular with collectors and print buyers. The streams and woodlands, teeming with life in spring and frozen in winter, were the source of countless canvases even long after he had moved away. His remarkable visual memory made it possible for him to carry these scenes in his head for translation to canvas in the years to come. Once when out painting the lilacs and apple trees in full bloom, Robert discovered he had left his canvas behind, so he painted on an extra palette. The small, lovely sketch remained in his third wife Caryl's collection until her death in March, 1980.

Two years of this rustic life in the woods proved enough for Robert who, in the words of his late wife, "began to yearn for the west coast again." He and Tula returned to the lovely, graceful coastal city of Laguna Beach, just south of Los Angeles;

Exhibit at Laguna Beach, Calif.

another art colony and one in which Robert rapidly rose to the front among his fellows. In the first year of his return, his painting "Golden Pacific" won the first prize in the Laguna Beach Art League's twenty-first annual exhibition. It was an appropriate and fitting "welcome home" present for him from the friends and associates he had nurtured a few years before.

But the times were full of upheavals, too. The early 1950's were memorable in several ways for Robert Wood and his career. He was divorced for the second time; he was nearly killed by an automobile; and he married for the third and final time.

Divorced from Tula in 1952 (she later married a Texas oilman after obtaining a gigantic settlement in her divorce from Robert, and died of cancer in 1967), the artist plunged even more feverishly into his work, turning out prize-winning landscapes and seascapes at an astonishing rate and solidifying his already lofty international reputation.

Robert had many close calls and brushes with death in his long and checquered career, but probably came closest to losing his life on Tuesday morning, January 6, 1953, when he was struck by a car at a crosswalk on a Laguna Beach street. Aged sixty-three at the time, he was in no condition to sustain so serious an injury. His right leg badly fractured, he lay on the hospital operating table for eight hours as doctors feverishly tried to set the mangled bones.

"They wanted to amputate the leg, but he wouldn't let them," Kitty revealed. "He told the doctors he was born with two legs and would die with two."

Robert's determination to keep both his legs was a smart decision. After he recovered, he did not even limp for the rest of his life.

Robert Wood always believed that good comes out of evil and proved it during his convalescence. One of his art students, herself a divorcee, Caryl Price, a pretty, vivacious brunette, took it upon herself to play Florence Nightingale to the stricken, crippled artist. She cooked and did laundry for her teacher, kept his house and studio clean, read to him and laughed at his constant flow of jokes and flirtatious jibes.

"You're going to need some looking after," she told the artist at his home after he had surgery on his leg.

"I couldn't advertise and find a prettier nurse," Robert replied, with that ever-present twinkle in his eye. "If I have you to look after me, I'm sorry I didn't bang up the other leg, too." Two days later, Caryl came in with a mischievous gleam in her own eye. "Look what I've found – an English cookbook. I'm going to try my hand at steak and kidney pie."

"Look out" Robert taunted playfully, "in my condition it wouldn't take much to kill me."

Playful teasing banter like this, coupled with Caryl's other kindnesses to the artist, soon led both to realize they had a unique and close rapport between them. Several months later they were husband and wife.

How did such a marriage come about? How did Caryl, some twenty years younger, win the heart of a man who was notorious for his appreciation of and charm over women and who remained a "ladies' man" to his dying day? It certainly wasn't due to there being a shortage of available women at the time. When Robert Wood wasn't chasing a pretty face (which wasn't often), a pretty face was chasing him. My son, Nelson, has an amusing anecdote to confirm this. He accompanied Robert to San Diego from his San Antonio visit in 1976 and tells how the artist flirted outrageously with a pretty, young stewardess on the flight. Before departing the plane, he talked her into giving him a ribbon from her hair, imploring: "My dear, I must have that ribbon!" And his affairs with women, during and between his three marriages, were numerous and colorful.

Caryl won him over with a combination of appealing qualities. During his convalescence, she learned to prepare a few of the English foods of which he was fond, and this certainly brought a special twinkle to his captivating eye. Since he was unable to paint, himself, he would invite Caryl to set up her easel in his room. He propped himself on pillows and gave her special, personal instruction to improve her craft, telling her: "My dear (his favorite expression to women), since I am unable to paint, we might as well do what we can to see you make progress."

Actually what "progressed" was a great measure of mutual love and trust. Robert realized that he had not only a pretty, bright helpful protege, but a woman who was in love with him and who was prepared to care for his needs in times of difficulty. Before his leg had healed, he popped the question in characteristic charming style, and his pupil promptly accepted. And although he never stopped flirting or turning his head at an attractive woman, his celebrated affairs of the heart ended when Caryl became Mrs. Wood.

With an artist for a wife, Robert moved into a new period of creativity which he shared generously with his spouse, whom he supported and encouraged constantly. They entered art competitions together and enjoyed many painting excursions in each other's company – to Palm Springs, the High Sierras, and the desert canyons of Arizona. They were a good-looking and dedicated "team," a quality Robert probably had always wanted in a wife without realizing it.

Nine years later, the Woods moved inland to the mountain climate of the High Sierras, near Bishop, California. Caryl continued her own painting career in earnest and conducted classes in art in her studio.

Robert's prints were by now selling in the tens of thousands annually, but he found himself getting further and further behind in requests for more originals. He simply could not meet the demand, fast as he was; but then, no artist could have.

Todd Watkins, who wrote the obituary notice on Robert Wood in the Inyo, California Register, the Bishop newspaper, said, "We enjoyed loafing in his studio while he painted and chatted. The man had a most brilliant mind and typically crisp British sense of humor. A very likeable man. He took great delight in associating with artist-producer Walter Lantz in recent years, helping Walter in refinements of landscape painting. He was proud to call the High Sierras his home. We were proud, indeed, to have known one of the most remarkable men of this or any century."

Walter Lantz, creator of Woody Woodpecker, one of the world's most popular animated film characters, in recent years

With wife Caryl in his studio – 1955

traveled to Bishop from his home on Silver Lake once a week to spend a day painting with Robert Wood. Walter was already a landscape artist and had several successful one-man shows, but he was delighted to learn more from the master, Robert Wood.

Of all the awards, prizes and honors that came his way during his California years, none pleased Robert Wood more than being commissioned by the American Express Company to paint a series of six scenes from America's National Parks. The company reproduced a limited edition of stunning serigraphs for its card-holding members and the series was one of the company's most outstanding sales promotions in the early 1970's.

"When American Express asked me to create a series of serigraphs exclusively for their card members," the artist wrote, "I was delighted. In serigraphy I could supervise reproduction of my paintings from start to finish."

Only 1,000 prints of each of the six paintings – probably the least number of prints ever made from a Wood original – were selected and Robert signed and numbered each. Today, these works are valuable collector's items, worth much more than the two hundred dollars they sold for when American Express issued them for its collection.

Less than four years later, with the artist now aged eighty-three, but still jaunty, witty and restless, the Woods moved again, this time to the coastal city of San Diego, where they bought a Victorian mansion badly in need of restoration. Caryl felt the increased heat and sunshine of this popular resort city would help alleviate a growing sinus problem, but it failed to do so, and Robert was clearly unhappy with his new address even though they made the house a showplace of elegance and taste. (When he visited me in San Antonio, he expressed his displeasure without mincing words: "I do not feel at home there.")

Robert and Caryl discovered that the huge Victorian three-story house had, like a giant shark, consumed so much time from their lives; precious time they should have been devoting to painting.

With one of his favorite cats.

Robert with Caryl and Violet, seated, 1974.

Caryl often lamented, in letters and conversations, about how little time she had to devote to her own artistic endeavors; but one could hardly expect her to have any, what with the endless moving to different houses, remodeling and decorating. The San Diego "experience" was a classic case in point.

It had been Caryl's dream to have that magnificent Victorian mansion completely restored to its original pristine state, but frustration met her at every turn. Everything, she said, was extremely difficult to find – not only good skilled workers, but materials. A simple piece of brass from a wonderful old cabinet, or just a doorknob could take days to search out.

Good-naturedly, of course, Robert had supported his wife's passion for decorating the splendid house. He was always helpful and deferential, but was so drawn into the project that he had little time for himself and his painting.

The house at the time was an unending circus of movement and noise – alive with painters, carpenters, plumbers, electricians. There was never an "escape hatch" to get away from the cacophony of confusion. Every time a hammer hit a nail, the noise reverberated throughout the house. The hammering and grinding were unceasing. Privacy, even for a moment, was non-existent.

Caryl had envisioned the total perfection of this beautiful century-old house, but soon she grew weary, knowing it was futile to hope her goal would ever be accomplished. Possibly the same thought occurred to Robert, but he was too much of a gentleman to say anything.

Caryl found herself "househunting" once again. When she had an appointment at the beauty salon, for example, she would allow herself an extra hour to look for a new home. This time she wanted a big, spacious house where she could have some precious peace and quiet. Obviously she wanted time to reflect and meditate, and both she and Robert needed a studio and the time to indulge their first love: Art.

One day she found it! The perfect house! It was a large rambling structure with lovely gracious gardens and a huge room that was perfect for a studio. But Caryl was apprehensive about broaching the subject to Robert; understandably, since he had already invested much time and even more money into the Victorian project. She planned her strategy carefully. The next morning she suggested they both have breakfast at a lovely English restaurant nearby. As they were enjoying muffins and marmalade, Caryl said softly: "Dearest, I want to move. We need more space, and I want a garden for flowers and fountains. I miss the birds and our quiet time on the patio – and especially our long talks. I have found a house I like very much. Would you look at it with me?"

Robert, ever gentle, patient and considerate, answered, "Whatever will make you happy, my dear, will make me happy."

It didn't take long to close the deal on the house and make the move to Miller Street. Boxes were unpacked again – the ones that originally had been packed in Bishop and stored. Finally there was room for everything.

In the new house Caryl was almost childlike; full of enthusiasm and brimming with ideas on decorating. So, once again, came the "parade" of carpenters to install a large skylight in the studio; painters and electricians. The noise started anew, but this time they didn't really mind because they had found a house that suited their needs so well. Also, this time she and Robert were able to paint while the workers were about because the studio was a separate structure. Caryl worked at one end of the large studio, and Robert at the other.

In the center of the studio was a table for a tea pot, and ever so often they would stop their labors at the easel to enjoy a cup of tea. They were delighted to be painting together again. Sometimes they would look at each other like newlyweds and hold their arms out to each other and embrace. Then they would go back to painting. Robert was eighty-three at the time.

I was overjoyed, to say the least, when Robert and Caryl invited me to come with Kitty from San Antonio for a visit to their new home. Frankly, I could not have been more thrilled if I had been invited by the President to the White House, or by the Queen to Buckingham Palace.

Kitty and I took a taxi from the airport to their house, and

Studio of Robert and Caryl. Caryl's space in foreground. San Diego, Calif.

I can't remember ever being more nervous and excited. Over and over I said to Kitty: "I can't believe this is happening to me!"

Only another artist can know the emotions I felt. The anticipation of finally meeting – in the flesh – the artist whom I most admired in my life, and actually being a guest in his home had me literally bursting with joy.

At last, after what seemed an eternity in the taxi, we arrived at the Woods' front door. There he was, waiting for us, with a big smile and those wonderful, luminous blue eyes.

Caryl had told us in a letter that Robert had been rather "frail," so I was pleasantly astonished to see a dapper, spry, vigorous, even youthful bundle of energy at the door. He even helped us get our luggage inside.

To this day I don't know what we said or did when we first met. All I can remember is my heart pounding wildly with the realization that, at last, here was my real-life hero – Robert Wood!

The stay in the Wood home, lasting about a week, was an experience to last a lifetime. They were the perfect hosts. Robert's pranks, jokes and fantastic stories kept us in stitches most of the time, and Caryl's quiet gracious demeanor was the perfect counterpoint. Kitty and I agreed completely that these two were "made" for each other.

Robert Wood, as he promised, paid a visit to me in the fall of 1976, five years after our initial communication and two years after my visit to San Diego. His visit to San Antonio was, if anything, more thrilling and unforgettable, and he fully lived up to his "advance billing."

Dapper, witty, playful, endlessly flirtatious, he charmed everyone in sight with his rapid-fire jokes, anecdotes and recollections of his colorful life as he described to his enthralled admirers – many of whom were artists – how he had to struggle to eke out a living when he first arrived in this country; how he criss-crossed the length and breadth of the land as a hobo; how he set up displays in paint store windows to peddle his instant "buckeye" pictures; on to the time he progressed to the complete self-confidence that enabled him finally to enter the

Arriving at San Antonio Airport with daughter Florence being greeted by Billy Beran, grandson and Maureen Tarazon, artist from London.

At airport pictured with Bruce and Debbie Sigoloff,
Violet and her mother, Rachel Wells.

world of serious painting. Famous Texas and regional artists descended on the Sigoloff Galleries where a reception for Robert was held on the occasion of a special display of his paintings. They fairly stood in awe at the small but commanding presence of the artist and practically "hung" on his every word. Most were astonished to see a man of his age with such vitality and love of life, along with such a quick and ready wit. (His sense of humor was evident when Kitty and I visited the Wood home in San Diego and Robert posed at a fireplace for publicity pictures, wearing unmatched shoes.)

About 400 artists, old friends and admirers turned out for the San Antonio reception, spilling all over the gallery and waiting in long lines outside. A public address system had to be used to urge those outside the gallery to be patient until they could be admitted inside. Through it all, Robert Wood never tired, never stopped joking, never stopped admiring the women. When he would greet one, he would ask, "Where have you been all my life?"

Many of the women visitors asked if they might kiss him, a suggestion that clearly delighted him. He kissed and autographed tirelessly right and left whenever they asked.

The reception was almost like a homecoming for his devoted disciples, the younger artists who had admired him from afar for so many years and who were now given the opportunity to talk to the legend in person.

"It was a thrill just to meet him," said Dalhart Windberg, a highly successful Texas oil master. "It was exciting to compare techniques and discussing art with him made the visit an unforgettable time."

A.D. Greer, another outstanding Texas artist, paid a visit to Robert while he was in San Antonio – a reunion that spanned many years. He was quick to acknowledge Robert Wood as the master who stands above them all, a sentiment that another landscape artist, W.A. Slaughter, would echo.

"Robert Wood is simply a fantastic artist and person," A.D. Greer said after his visit. "He is great, and that is all one can say."

Nearly everyone who came under the influence of Robert

Autographing a painting.

Wood during his colorful life, whether or not he was an admirer of his paintings, confessed the same thing: he was an unforgettable man. And his puckish sense of humor never failed to impress those around him. Once, during a lull in conversation, Robert winked at his wife and said, "I always wondered why such a looker as you married an old goat like me." Several times, in letters and conversations, Robert referred to himself as "the old goat."

He may have been an "old goat," but it was a fast goat, to be sure. For one thing that never left Robert Wood was his celebrated speed at rendering a canvas. In a note dated July 13, 1972 (the artist was eighty-two) he wrote: "Yesterday at 3:00 p.m. I had a phone call from my publisher in New York. He needs an ocean scene, 18x24, right away. Deadline of July 20. It is drying in the hot house at present. Will be mailed at 5:00 p.m."

And his works continued to mount in value prodigiously. An Atlanta art dealer, Dr. Carlton Palmer, wrote me in a letter of August 5, 1972: "A gallery in San Angelo, Texas just sold a Robert Wood 25x30 autumn landscape for $4,000. It is the one we sold twenty-five years ago for $375."

Where he found the time to dash off so many notes and letters, no one can say. But he was a charming correspondent. One of his letters which I cherish came from Bishop and was dated January 30, 1972 in which he described a former house in Laguna Beach: "We were only a few feet from the Catholic Church and sold it to them for the priests to live in. We had a pair of Siamese cats who would go in the church during services and frustrate the Monsignor so that he would forget his sermon...the cats would drink the holy water and come home crossing themselves; when I asked one of the churchgoers how they made holy water, he told me they boil the hell out of it."

He remained to the last an "improvisational" man, cooking up surprises on the spur of the moment. When visiting me and staying in my San Antonio home for nearly three weeks (and painting five large canvases) he drifted into a conversation about art with my son, Bruce, who was delighted that Robert showed

Painting "The Homestead," pictured in color section.

so much interest in him.

"Do you paint?" Robert asked him.

"A little," was my son's reply.

"Let's paint; I'll show you how."

This was very exciting to all of us. Bruce said, "Any time while you're here, I'd be very happy to watch you paint."

"What's wrong with right now?" asked the artist.

Bruce said with astonishment, "Do you mean right now?"

"Now," said Robert.

The next few seconds were pandemonium as Bruce and I kept bumping into each other getting the studio cleared and paints and easels set up.

Having the artist stay in my home was an unforgettable memory. At frequent intervals I would waken during the night with a feeling of awe as I pondered the fact that the great Robert Wood was asleep upstairs in my own house!

Robert Wood thoroughly enjoyed his return to Texas and San Antonio, and mentioned to several people that it felt like "coming home." Of course, the city was much changed from when he last saw it in 1941, some 35 years before. Yet, there was much that was familiar to him, too, and he recalled with fondness a few of the downtown landmarks that were still there – the River Walk, where he spent many a lazy afternoon in the 1920's, sketching and resting; Casa Rio, where his studio was located when he was just getting started in San Antonio; the famous Schilo's Delicatessen on Commerce Street, where he and Porfirio Salinas often enjoyed lunch. Especially he enjoyed dining at the historic and famous St. Anthony Hotel which was, and is still, one of the city's most prestigious addresses.

"In some ways," he observed to me, "lots of places look like they did when I was here, except the prices have gone out of sight. But nearly everything else has changed, as it has everywhere else. It's still a beautiful city and I didn't realize how much I had missed it."

Robert and Caryl decided soon that their former life in Bishop was far better than their present condition in the noisy, rapidly growing climate of San Diego. Robert missed the majestic

In gallery with Violet and son Nelson Sigoloff, who accompanied Robert back to California from San
Antonio.

William Edward Beran, only grandchild of Robert
Wood.

mountain peaks, the clear unpolluted air and the more relaxed life-style that was conducive to artistic expression. And so, in mid-1976, with Robert now aged eighty-seven, the couple moved again, and for the last time. They were able to purchase an ideal location for two artists: a spacious comfortable house with a studio for each. From the house's rear window, Robert could gaze at the subtle beauties of Mount Tom, one of his all-time favorite sights and which he translated to canvas many times and in many moods. Here he remained, serene and confident, until his death three years later.

Mount Tom, in fact, was something of an American symbol for Robert Wood. Its unchanging strength and solidity, its singular, proud beauty was, for the artist, a picture of Nature at her finest and most complete state. And so, it was appropriate that following a simple, dignified Christian Science funeral service, Robert Wood's ashes were scattered across his beloved Mount Tom.

How Robert Wood Painted

How did Robert Wood paint? In style, one could not call him either a Realist or an Abstractionist. The truth lies somewhere in between. He sought, always, to get at the "heart" of his subject, whether it was a canyon in Arizona, a field of bluebonnets in Texas, a frozen lake in upstate New York, or a seascape on a Pacific slope.

He approached his art as he approached life itself, with a profound wonder and respect; an almost childlike love and awe of what he called "God's handiwork." A simple spring flower, tossing its tiny head in the breeze from an enormous field of larger, more colorful blossoms moved him as much as the sweeping vistas of the Grand Canyon. He saw the hand of the Creator wherever he turned and he tried, in his painting, to capture just this atmosphere and the eternal truths and beauties of Nature without distortion. He wanted to be an interpreter of Nature, not a literal commentator.

Billy's daughter, Brandee Nicole Beran only great grandchild of Robert Wood.

True to his nature, he always strived to keep his touch "light" and distinctive. He would counsel his students: "Don't take yourself too seriously, or your painting either, and both of you will turn out better."

Above all, Robert Wood, in his personal approach to painting and in his classes, stressed two things: simplicity and honesty. He felt that a young painter, even with modest talent, would go far if he adhered to these two basic principles.

"Don't think you can do a masterpiece on your first or second try. Please be reasonable with yourself."

"Enjoy painting. All you feel as you paint will be reflected in your work.

"Painting is a joyful experience. So – have fun."

The Palette Of Robert Wood

AC	Alizarin Crimson	IB	Ivory Black
BM	Brown Madder	NY	Naples Yellow
BMA	Brown Madder Alizarin	PB	Prussian Blue
BS	Burnt Sienna	RS	Raw Sienna
BU	Burnt Umber	SG	Sap Green
CB	Cerulean Blue	UMB	Ultramarine Blue
CO	Cadmium Orange	VIR	Viridian Blue
CoB	Cobalt Blue	VDB	Van Dyke Brown
CoG	Chromium Oxide Green	W	White
CRL	Cadmium Red Lightest	YO	Yellow Ochre
CYD	Cadmium Yellow Deep	YZ	Yellow Zinc
CYL	Cadmium Yellow Light	PW	Permalba White
CYM	Cadmium Yellow Medium		

At easel. Studio in Bishop.

Robert Wood's Painting Notes

General Rules, Terminology, Techniques

Generally, never mix more than three colors
Pat on paint with heel of brush
Get back and view painting from distance every 20 minutes
Cohesion: Two wet paints sticking together
Patience: Do not hurry!
Always cut in rather than paint into object (sky cut
  into trees)
Those who can, DO. Those who can't, TEACH
Brown Sauce School: Darks mostly from Europe
For distant, lacy trees, pat in with large brush
Lead poisoning: Painter's colic
Never put too much texture into sky
Seascape back water laid in with smaller strokes
Generally use warm undercoating for seascape sky
Always less detail in distant trees or mountains
Generally warm the bottom of a breaking wave
Never paint things as "cool" as you see them
Scratch in heavy grass or water with end of brush
Small leaves: Use small sable brush
Reflected lights are as important as highlights
Don't flare butts of trees too much
Paint with natural or fluorescent light

When starting on a dry painting, coat with Medium

Always add Yellow Ochre to yellows to cut brashy effect

Tie things together: Grass into rocks, limbs into limbs, etc.

For distant twig effect, scratch with end of brush

Roll brush: That's why they are round

Fallen leaves: Texture first with dark, then dry.
   Then scumble on.

Generally paint tree limbs up or down at 45 degrees

Tree reflections: Short, vertical strokes

Hold paint brush like it is going to fall out of your hand

Crawling paint: When paint does not adhere to canvas

Mix paint on canvas as much as possible

There is always more Green in fall scenes than you realize

Never use pure white or black − add a color to each

Try to use Burnt Umber instead of black

Don't get leaves too sharp

Foam holes in surf larger than in front

Slightly blue the edges of distant trees

Flowers in foreground with heavy texture to make
   stand up

Reflections in smooth water: Like a mirror

Use extreme highlights to last of painting

As you come forward, color, contrast and detail intensify

Use Compound S-curves

Generally use Yellow Ochre in tree greens

Seascape sand; both warm and cool colors

Sky always darker at top than at bottom

Shadow: Use the darkest component of the object
   shadowed

Foreground shadow more intense

Reflections never the same intensity as the thing reflected

Usually try to make one strong horizontal line and a
   vertical line

Center of interest ⅓ in from sides

Try to use odd numbers of objects (1,3,5 trees, etc.)

Cadmium colors: Gives life to color mixture

Don't overdo highlights

To darken a color, add the darkest component of the
  mixture

In spring scenes, do not overdo the bright greens

Name signature should be small; use a No. 4 round sable

Reds are powerful colors – use sparingly

Zinc Yellow makes White look whiter than it is

Use more detail in base of distant mountains

In forest paint light shafts behind trees for more depth

Use complementary colors for "punch"

To gray any color, use its complementary

Usually the darkest part of a tree foliage is in center
  of tree

Overbrushing on canvas scrubs the life out of paint

Use rags for glazing or wiping painting instead of paper
  towels

Use complementary colors for contrast as well as shadows

Soften the edge of shadows

Avoid bright colors at edge of painting

Sketch painting with charcoal, pencil or diluted blue paint

Seldom use colors straight out of tube

Get three light values from everything you paint

Glaze distant mountains for atmosphere effect with
  blue-white

Don't overwork rocks

Alizarin Crimson and Ultramarine Blue good glazing colors

Alizarin Crimson and Ultramarine Blue are transparent
  colors; good for shadows

Shadows are usually thinner than the object shadowed

Have animals looking into the painting

Usually paint toward yourself (sky first)

If nothing goes right, set aside and get to it another day

Try to have three or four paintings going at the same time
  (some drying)

Do not use dryers in your painting

Media: 1/2 Linseed Oil and 1/2 Turpentine

Receding colors grayed with complementary

Skies (on Seascapes)

BLUE   Add Cadmium Red Lightest
Cobalt Blue to White

WHITE   Add Yellow Ochre and Cadmium
Red Light for warmth

BLUE   Add Prussian Blue to White
Naples Yellow
Cadmium Red Light
White for hot spot

As you work, use:

Cadmium Orange and Cobalt Blue and
White for clouds

WARM GRAY SKY:

WHITE   Cobalt blue and
Burnt Sienna
Cadmium Yellow Light

Skies (Sunny)

To paint sun:

WHITE   Naples Yellow

To outline sun:

     Yellow Ochre, Cadmium Red
Light, White

Hot spot:

     Work with Yellow Ochre,
Cadmium Red Light (Juicy)
With same brush, add
Cobalt Blue, Burnt Sienna

Clouds:

     Cadmium Yellow Light
Yellow Ochre

Skies
(for Mountain and Bluebonnet Scenes)

WHITE   Cadmium Red Light
            Cobalt Blue

WHITE   Cerulean Blue with touch of
            Alizarin Crimson

WHITE   Naples Yellow
            Work light to dark, then mix
            Cadmium Red Light and
            Yellow Ochre for dark, gray sky
            Work Prussian Blue into White
            for normal gray sky

Edge of cloud:

            Cadmium Red Light
            Cadmium Yellow Deep
            White

Dark of cloud:

Cadmium Red Light
Yellow Ochre
White (use sparingly)

Skies (Bottom)

            Yellow Ochre, Cadmium Red Light
            (thick like butter)
            Prussian blue
            (work in from top)

Skies (for Snow Scenes)

Dark in sky:

  Burnt sienna
  Cobalt blue

Highlights (cloud):

  Cadmium Red Light
  White, with a little
  Cadmium Yellow Deep

BLUE Cerulean Blue
  White
  Prussian Blue

Hot spot:

  Cadmium Red Light
  White
  Cobalt Blue (work into hot spot)

Skies (bright)

  White
  Naples Yellow
  Cadmium Red Light

Skies (green)

  Viridian Blue
  Cadmium Yellow Light

  White
  Prussian blue
  (add as you work)

Trees

Foliage, evergreens

Ivory Black
Cadmium Yellow Light
  Highlight Light into wet Van Dyke Brown and
  Sap Green. In spring use a little 3 Y darks:
  Brown Madder, Ivory Black or Ivory Black and
  Alizarin Crimson or Viridian and Burnt Sienna.
  Lighten with Cadmium Yellow Light

Foreground

Viridian
Burnt Sienna
Cadmium Yellow Medium

Darks:

Cadmium Red Dark
Sap Green or Viridian
Burnt Sienna
Cadmium Yellow Medium
Cadmium Orange
Cobalt Blue

Trees
(Trunks and Limbs)

Burnt Sienna
Cobalt Blue
White (half light)
Burnt Sienna
Cadmium Yellow Deep
White

Highlight:

Naples Yellow
Cadmium Yellow

Distant trunks:

>Add White or Ivory Black to above
>or Yellow Ochre, Burnt Sienna,
>Cobalt Blue and White
>Van Dyke Brown
>Yellow Ochre
>White
>(same mixture for branch)
>Van Dyke Brown (under branch)
>Alizarin

Half light:

>Brown Madder
>Alizarin
>Yellow Ochre
>White

Highlight:

>Yellow Ochre
>Cadmium Yellow Deep
>White

Trees
(Redwoods)

>Cadmium Red Light
>Cadmium Orange
>Cadmium Yellow Deep

Darks:

>Van Dyke Brown
>Ultramarine Blue or Brown Madder, Burnt Sienna
>Cadmium Orange
> add Ultramarine Blue for dark fall tree color
>Cadmium Red Light
>Burnt Sienna

Desert Smoke Tree

>Cobalt Blue
>Yellow Gray

Oaks

Yellow Ochre
Chromium Oxide Green
Cadmium Red Light

Birch (Foliage)

Speckle with Naples Yellow
  for shimmering effect

Fir (Trunks)

Brown Madder
Alizarin
Cobalt Blue
White

Branches:

Brown Madder
Yellow Ochre
White

Green on trunks:

Chromium Oxide Green
  (lace with fine brush)

Ground

Burnt Sienna
Naples Yellow
Cadmium Red Light

Forest Road:

Burnt Sienna
Naples Yellow
Cadmium Red Light

Highlight:

Naples Yellow
Burnt Sienna

Forest path:

> Burnt Sienna
> Ultramarine Blue
> White

Desert sand:

> Yellow Ochre
> White

Dark ground:

> Yellow Ochre
> White
> Cadmium Red Medium
> Pure Yellow Ochre for dark areas

Roads (horizontal strokes):

> Yellow Ochre
> White

Shadow:

> Blue, Purple, Gray

Snow

Bright:

> Cerulean

Background:

> Cadmium Orange
> Blue
>   (gray effect)
>   for more violet effect
>   add Alizarin Crimson

Highlights:

> Cadmium Red
> Naples Yellow
> White or Zinc Yellow

Shadow:

>Cerulean blue
>Alizarin Crimson or
>Cobalt blue and Alizarin Crimson

Water

Distant gray:

>Alizarin Crimson
>Viridian

Dark green waves:

>Cadmium Yellow Light
>Ivory Black
> or
>Viridian
>Ivory Black
>Raw Sienna

Wavelets in foam:

>Viridian
>Raw Sienna
>
>(Foam holes larger in front; make surf edge dark
>first, then lay in blue-white foam to edge)

Foam hot spot:

>Alizarin Crimson
>Cadmium Red Light

Wave crest (luminous):

>Chromium Oxide
>Green and White

Grass, Rocks

Golden grass:

>Burnt Sienna
>Zinc Yellow
>White

Mountain rocks:

> Ultramarine Blue
> Yellow Ochre

Highlight:

> Yellow Ochre
> White

Flowers

Bluebonnets:
Distant flowers:

> Cobalt Blue
> Alizarin Crimson
> White
> (Start with half-tones, then darks; mix Cobalt Blue
> half-tones with Alizarin Crimson laid on flat)

Flowers (Heavy, thick foreground)
Dark shadows on edge of flowers:

> Alizarin Crimson
> Cobalt Blue

Hot spot into darker flowers:

> White
> Cobalt Blue
> Alizarin Crimson

Green foliage around flowers

> Viridian
> Burnt Sienna
> (Work horizontally into flowers, lighten with Cad-
> mium Yellow Light)

Poppies:

> Cadmium Yellow Dark
> Cadmium Orange (do not mix)
>   (Dot Naples Yellow into edge of poppy)

Desert Verbena:

> Alizarin Crimson
> Cadmium Red Light

Darks:

> Alizarin Crimson and Viridian
>   streaked into flowers
> (Scramble Alizarin and White over background
> Verbenas, and lightly over foreground Verbenas)

Color Plates

1. Beside The Still Water – 24x36 – painted in 1972 – Private Collection
2. The Homestead – 30x40 – painted in 1976
3. Winter – 8x10
4. Autumn Serenity – 24x30 – Painted in 1976 as a gift to Violet.
5. Golden Autumn – 11x14
6. Bluebonnet Time in Texas – 24x36
7. Autumn In The Catskills – 24x36
8. Mountain Retreat – 16x20
9. The Last Mountain – 12x16 – Painted in 1979
10. Laguna Shores – 24x48
11. Ocean Sunset – 16x20
12. White Birches – 30x36 – Circa 1930 – Collection of Mr. & Mrs. Harold Herndon
13. April Showers – 18x24 – Personalized on back of canvas. "To my grandson Billy from Robert Wood."
14. Majesty – 11x14 – Personalized on back of canvas, to Bruce Sigoloff, "To My Friend Bruce from Robert Wood
15. Brazos River – 18x24 – Collection of Mr. and Mrs. Elmer Dobbins.
16. Sunrise on Mt. Tom – 18x24 – Collection of Dr. and Mrs. Duncan Poth.
17. The First Snow – 24x36 – Collection of Mr. & Mrs. George Musselman.

1. Beside The Still Water – 24x36 – painted in 1972 –
Private Collection

2. The Homestead – 30x40 – painted in 1976

3. Winter – 8x10

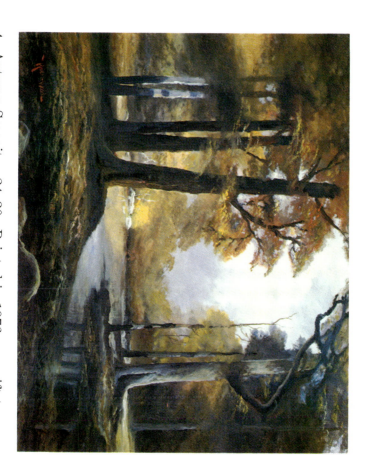

4. Autumn Serenity – 24x30 – Painted in 1976 as a gift to Violet.

5. Golden Autumn — 11x14

6. Bluebonnet Time in Texas – 24x36

7. Autumn In The Catskills – 24x36

8. Mountain Retreat – 16x20

9. The Last Mountain – 12x16 – Painted in 1979

10. Laguna Shores – 24x48

11. Ocean Sunset — 16x20 — Collection of Mrs. & Mrs. Robert Hausser

12. White Birches – 30x36 – Circa 1930 – Collection of Mr. &
Mrs. Harold Herndon

13. April Showers – 18x24 – Personalized on back of canvas. "To my grandson Billy from Robert Wood."

14. Majesty – 11x14 – Personalized on back of canvas, to Bruce Sigoloff, "To My Friend Bruce from Robert Wood

15. Brazos River—18x24—Collection of Mr. and Mrs. Elmer Dobbins.

16. Sunrise on Mt. Tom – 18x24 – Collection of Dr. and Mrs. Duncan Poth.

17. The First Snow—24x36—Collection of Mr. & Mrs. George Musselman.